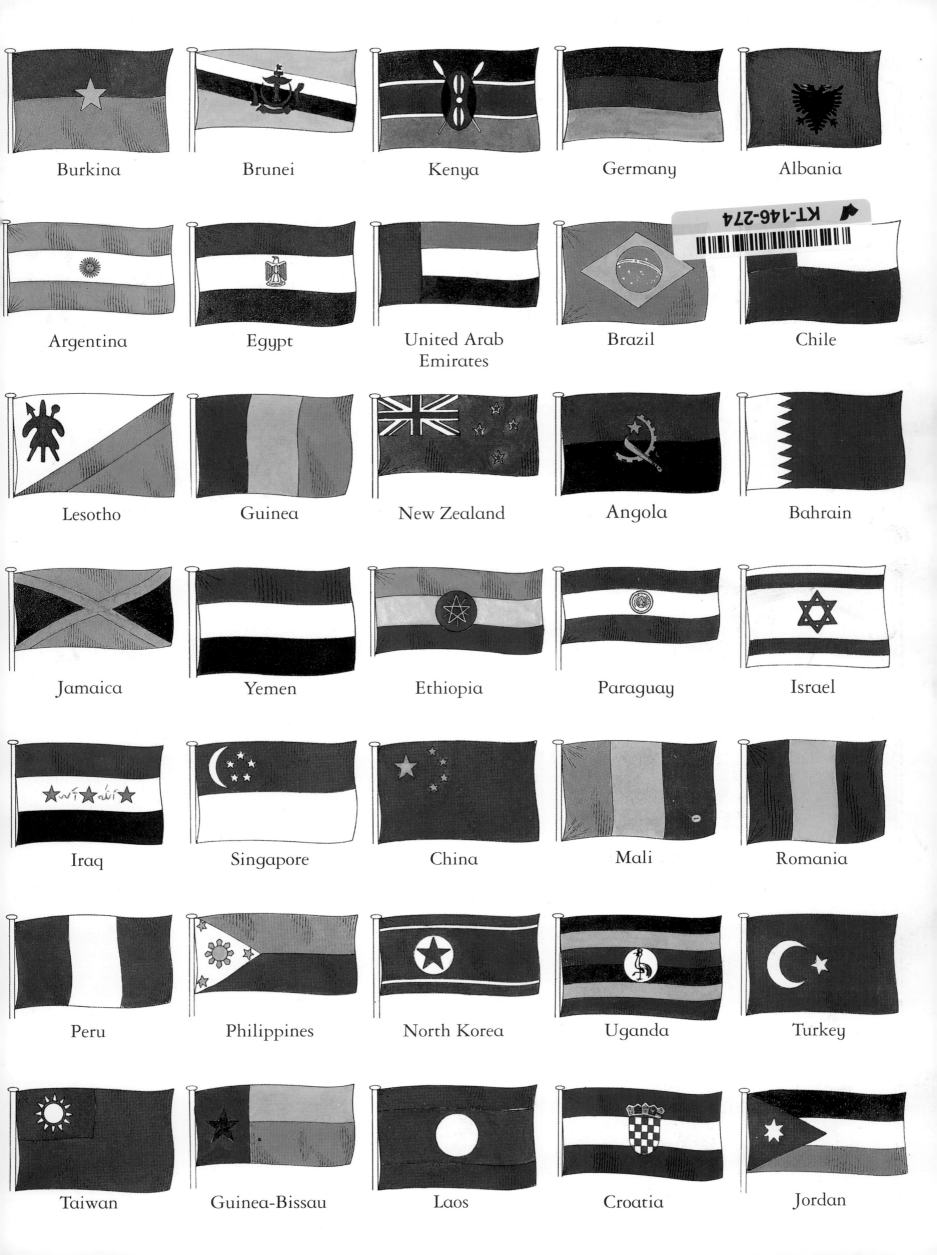

Burkina	Brunei	Kenya	Germany	Albania
Argentina	Egypt	United Arab Emirates	Brazil	Chile
Lesotho	Guinea	New Zealand	Angola	Bahrain
Jamaica	Yemen	Ethiopia	Paraguay	Israel
Iraq	Singapore	China	Mali	Romania
Peru	Philippines	North Korea	Uganda	Turkey
Taiwan	Guinea-Bissau	Laos	Croatia	Jordan

KT-146-274

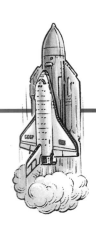

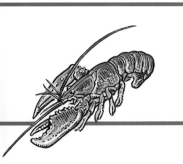

DK First Atlas

Written by Bill Boyle

Illustrated by Dave Hopkins

DK

LONDON • NEW YORK • SYDNEY • DELHI

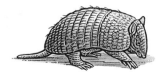

www.dk.com

Note to Parents

DK First Atlas has been specially designed to introduce young children to the countries and continents of the world and to the language of maps. By looking at the colourful picture maps and photographs, children will develop an understanding of the different regions of the world and their distinctive features. For each region, children will find out whether the climate is hot or cold, where the rivers or mountains are, where people live and work, the crops that farmers grow, and the plants and animals that inhabit the area. These features will enable children to build a wider view of the world by comparing the differences between countries.

Each double page offers many topics for discussion. Open-ended questions will stimulate children to talk about and use each picture map and help them to locate places in the world. A journey line is marked in red across each map. As children trace each imaginary journey, they will gain information about what they might see on a visit to each part of the world. The journey box on each map estimates the time it would take to travel the route by plane or car, introducing children to a sense of scale and distance.

The introductory section of this book aims to explain to children what maps are, and how and why we use them. Maps and the information they contain are starting points in a child's explorations. *DK First Atlas* is the ideal book to encourage children to want to find out more about our amazing planet.

Bill Boyle   Author

Project Editors Monica Byles, Fran Jones
Art Editor Peter Radcliffe
Managing Editor Jane Yorke
Managing Art Editor Chris Scollen
Production Ruth Cobb
Cartographic Research Roger Bullen
Picture Research Catherine O'Rourke

Editor's Note
Only the national flag of each country is shown on the endpapers of this book.

First published in Great Britain in 1994
by Dorling Kindersley Limited,
9 Henrietta Street, London WC2E 8PS
Reprinted 1995 (twice), 1996, 1997, 1998 (twice), 1999
Copyright © 1994, 1999 Dorling Kindersley Limited, London

All rights reserved. No part of this publication may be reproduced, stored in a retrieval system, or transmitted in any form or by any means, electronic, mechanical, photocopying, recording or otherwise, without the prior written permission of the copyright owner.

A CIP catalogue record for this book is available from the British Library.

ISBN 0-7513-6306-5

Reproduced by Classicscan, Singapore
Printed and bound in Italy by L.E.G.O.

Contents

Our world

We live on a planet called the Earth, which is a huge ball of rock, floating in space. The Earth, our world, is always turning, but we cannot feel it moving.

Our world looks flat from the ground or from the air, but in fact it is round. We know this because people have travelled into space and taken photographs of our planet.

The Solar System
The Earth is one of a family of nine planets that travel around a star called the Sun. Together, these planets are called the Solar System. Can you name the planets that are closest to the Earth? Which planet is furthest from the Sun?

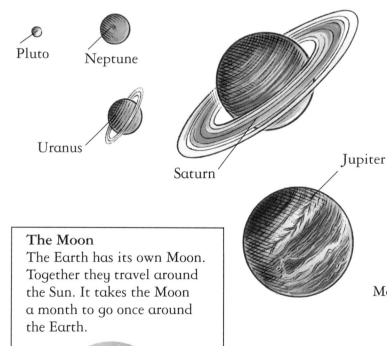

Pluto
Neptune
Uranus
Saturn
Jupiter

The Sun
The Sun is a million times larger than the Earth. This gigantic ball of hot gases and fire gives out warmth and light. The Earth takes a whole year, or 365 days, to travel once around the Sun.

Moon   Earth
Mars
Mercury
Venus

Sun

The Moon
The Earth has its own Moon. Together they travel around the Sun. It takes the Moon a month to go once around the Earth.

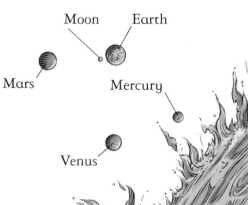

The Earth in space

This is a space satellite photograph of the Earth. It shows that most of the planet is covered in sea. Look closely at the land. Can you tell where there are rivers, lakes, or mountains?

Space satellite
A space satellite is a machine that travels in outer space, collecting and sending information to our planet.

Looking at the Earth

The Earth is so large that you can only see its round shape from far out in space. From this distance, you can only recognize the shapes of the land and the sea.

Inside the Earth

People live on the outer part of the Earth, which is called the crust. This picture shows the Earth with a piece cut out, so that you can see what the inside looks like.

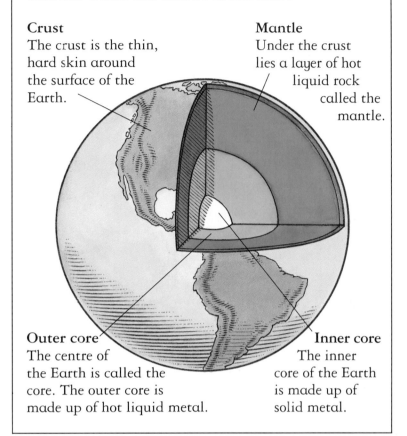

Crust
The crust is the thin, hard skin around the surface of the Earth.

Mantle
Under the crust lies a layer of hot liquid rock called the mantle.

Outer core
The centre of the Earth is called the core. The outer core is made up of hot liquid metal.

Inner core
The inner core of the Earth is made up of solid metal.

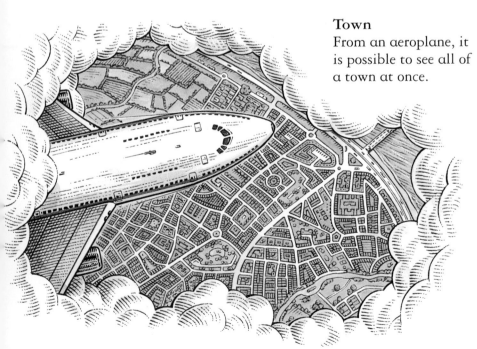

Town
From an aeroplane, it is possible to see all of a town at once.

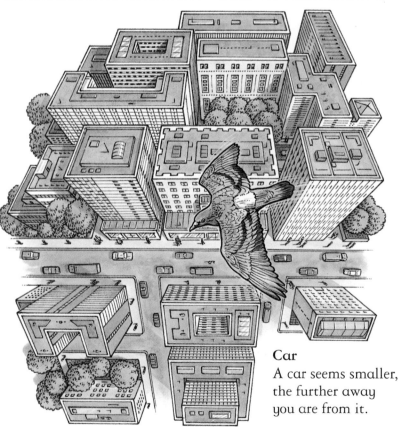

Car
A car seems smaller, the further away you are from it.

View from a plane

Have you ever looked down from the window of an aeroplane? Some things on the ground are so tiny that you cannot see them. Fields, towns, roads, and rivers look like patterns.

View from a building

Have you ever looked down from the top of a hill or a tall building? From this height, everything looks much smaller. Even large cars look like toys in the streets far below.

What is an atlas?

An atlas is a book of maps or picture information about the world. It shows you the shapes and sizes of parts of the land and sea, and also names them. The maps on these two pages show that land is divided into large areas called continents, while the sea is divided into oceans.

World map

This is a flat map of our round world. The map shows all seven continents at once. Which continent do you live in?

Globe

The Earth spins around an invisible pole, which is called the North Pole at the top, and the South Pole at the bottom. A globe is a round map of the world.

North Pole

Equator

South Pole

The Equator

The Earth is divided by an imaginary line called the Equator, exactly halfway between the North and South Poles. It is hot all year round near the Equator. The further you are from the Equator, the colder it is.

Compass

Most maps include a North point. If you know where North is, you can find out where you are.

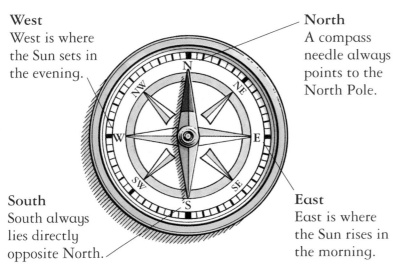

West
West is where the Sun sets in the evening.

North
A compass needle always points to the North Pole.

South
South always lies directly opposite North.

East
East is where the Sun rises in the morning.

Countries

Each continent, except for Australia and Antarctica, is made up of several countries, where people live under different rules and speak different languages.

South America

The continent of South America is made up of 13 different countries.

Map colours

Each country is shown in a different colour to help you read the map.

10

North and South America
The continent of North America is joined to South America. Together, the two continents stretch most of the way from the North Pole to the South Pole.

Europe
Europe is one of the smallest continents.

Africa
The continent of Africa is joined to Asia.

Asia
Asia is the largest continent.

EUROPE

ASIA

ATLANTIC OCEAN

AFRICA

PACIFIC OCEAN

Equator

Australia
Australia is the smallest continent. It is surrounded by several island countries.

SOUTH AMERICA

AUSTRALIA

SOUTHERN OCEAN

Antarctica
Antarctica is the cold, icy continent around the South Pole.

ANTARCTICA

Country borders

Borders mark the line where one country ends and another country begins. Some countries share natural borders, such as a river, lake, or range of mountains.

Natural border
This photo shows the Himalayan mountain range that divides the countries of China and India.

Scale

A world map is a small picture of our enormous world. The countries are shown at the right size, or scale, in relation to each other. The scale on a map helps you to work out how far apart places are.

Flying around the world

If you flew non-stop around the world, it would take you more than two days, flying at a speed of 800 km per hour (800 km/h) or 500 miles per hour (500 mph).

Driving around the world
If you could drive non-stop around the world, it would take you about three weeks, driving at a speed of 80 km/h (50 mph).

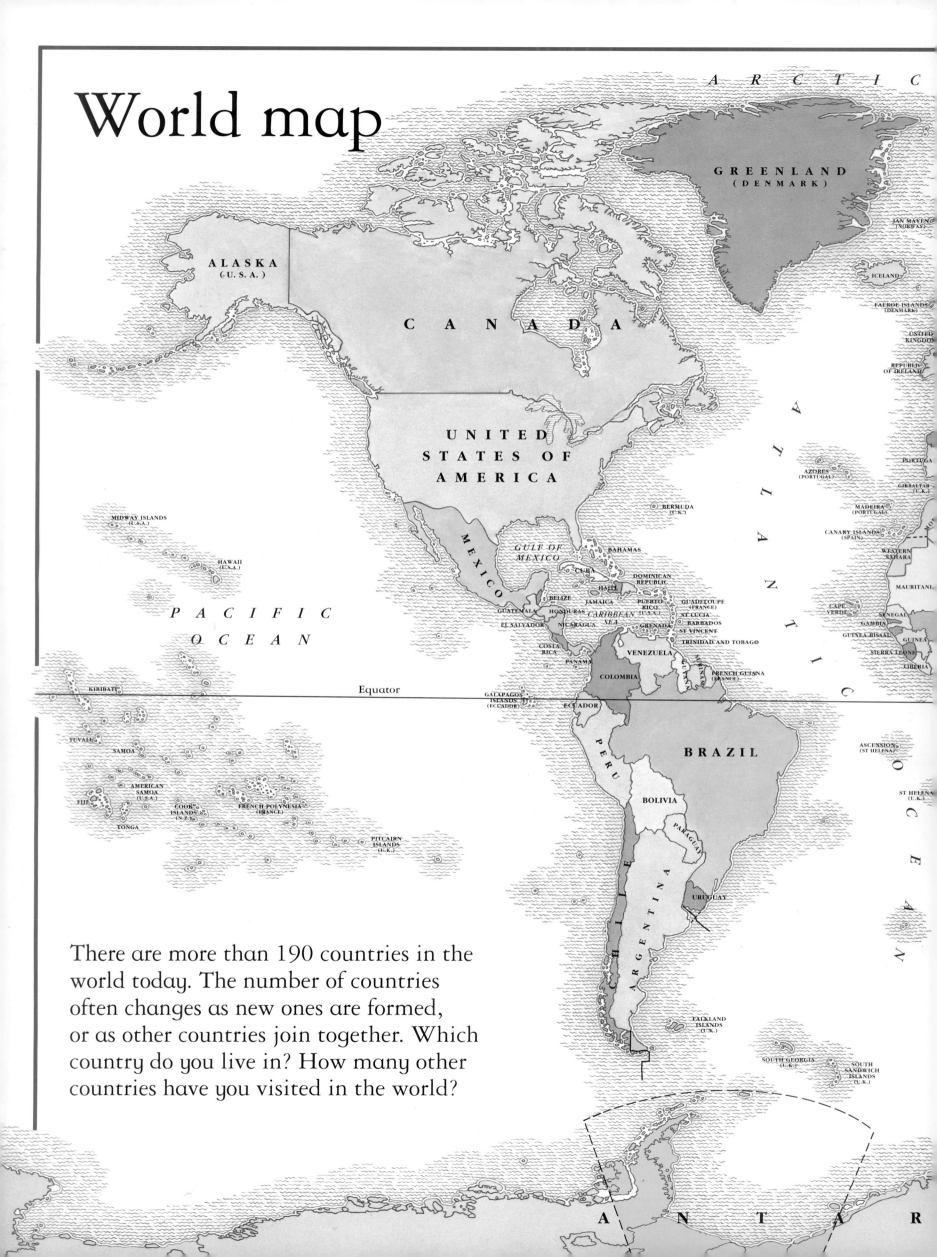

World map

A R C T I C

GREENLAND
(DENMARK)

JAN MAYEN
(NORWAY)

ICELAND

FAEROE ISLANDS
(DENMARK)

UNITED
KINGDOM

REPUBLIC
OF IRELAND

ALASKA
(U.S.A.)

C A N A D A

A T L A N T I C

PORTUGAL

AZORES
(PORTUGAL)

GIBRALTAR
(U.K.)

UNITED
STATES OF
AMERICA

BERMUDA
(U.K.)

MADEIRA
(PORTUGAL)

CANARY ISLANDS
(SPAIN)

WESTERN
SAHARA

MIDWAY ISLANDS
(U.S.A.)

M
E
X
I
C
O

GULF OF
MEXICO

BAHAMAS

CUBA

MAURITANIA

HAWAII
(U.S.A.)

HAITI

DOMINICAN
REPUBLIC

PUERTO
RICO
(U.S.A.)

GUADELOUPE
(FRANCE)

CAPE
VERDE

SENEGAL

P A C I F I C

O C E A N

BELIZE

GUATEMALA

HONDURAS

JAMAICA

CARIBBEAN
SEA

ST LUCIA

BARBADOS

GAMBIA

GUINEA-BISSAU

GUINEA

EL SALVADOR

NICARAGUA

GRENADA

ST VINCENT

TRINIDAD AND TOBAGO

SIERRA LEONE

LIBERIA

COSTA
RICA

PANAMA

VENEZUELA

FRENCH GUIANA
(FRANCE)

KIRIBATI

Equator

COLOMBIA

GALAPAGOS
ISLANDS
(ECUADOR)

ECUADOR

ASCENSION
(ST HELENA)

TUVALU

SAMOA

P E R U

B R A Z I L

AMERICAN
SAMOA
(U.S.A.)

BOLIVIA

ST HELENA
(U.K.)

FIJI

COOK
ISLANDS
(N.Z.)

FRENCH POLYNESIA
(FRANCE)

TONGA

PARAGUAY

PITCAIRN
ISLANDS
(U.K.)

C
H
I
L
E

A
R
G
E
N
T
I
N
A

URUGUAY

C

E

A

N

There are more than 190 countries in the
world today. The number of countries
often changes as new ones are formed,
or as other countries join together. Which
country do you live in? How many other
countries have you visited in the world?

FALKLAND
ISLANDS
(U.K.)

SOUTH GEORGIA
(U.K.)

SOUTH
SANDWICH
ISLANDS
(U.K.)

A N T A R

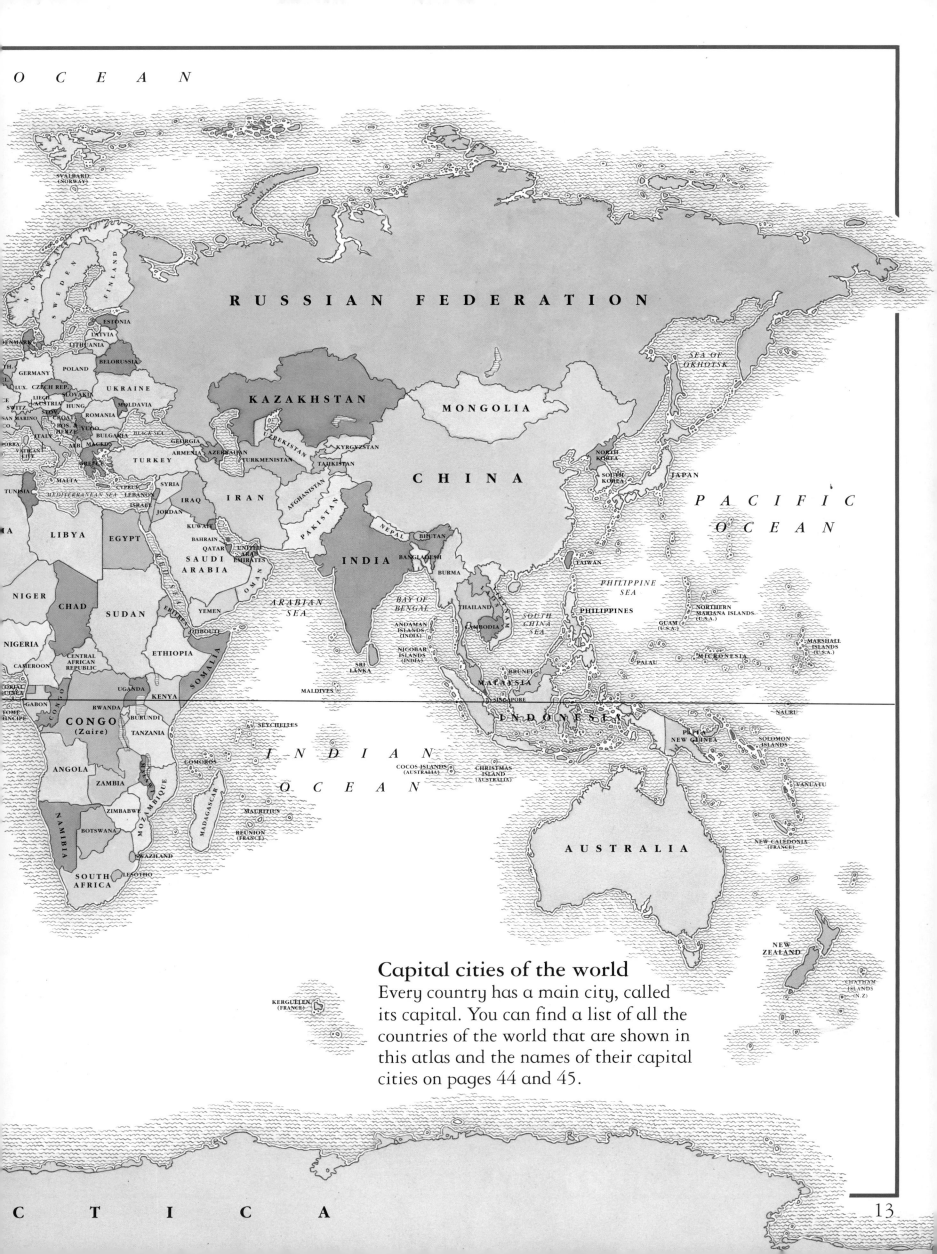

OCEAN

SVALBARD
(NORWAY)

RUSSIAN FEDERATION

SEA OF
OKHOTSK

NORWAY
SWEDEN
FINLAND
ESTONIA
LATVIA
LITHUANIA
DENMARK
GERMANY POLAND
BELORUSSIA
LUX. CZECH REP.
SLOVAKIA
LIECH.
SWITZ. AUSTRIA HUNG.
SAN MARINO SLOV.
BOS. & CROATIA
ITALY HERZE. YUGO.
VATICAN CITY
ROMANIA
MOLDAVIA
BULGARIA
MACED.
ALB.
GREECE
BLACK SEA
GEORGIA
ARMENIA AZERBAIJAN
TURKEY
MALTA
TUNISIA
MEDITERRANEAN SEA
CYPRUS
LEBANON
SYRIA
ISRAEL

UKRAINE

KAZAKHSTAN

MONGOLIA

UZBEKISTAN
KYRGYZSTAN
TURKMENISTAN
TAJIKISTAN

CHINA

NORTH
KOREA
SOUTH
KOREA

JAPAN

PACIFIC
OCEAN

LIBYA
EGYPT
NIGER
CHAD
SUDAN
NIGERIA
CAMEROON
CENTRAL
AFRICAN
REPUBLIC
EQUATORIAL
GUINEA
GABON
SÃO TOMÉ
& PRINCIPE
CONGO
(Zaire)
RWANDA
BURUNDI
TANZANIA
UGANDA
KENYA
SOMALIA
ETHIOPIA
DJIBOUTI
ERITREA
YEMEN
OMAN
SAUDI
ARABIA
BAHRAIN
QATAR
UNITED
ARAB
EMIRATES
KUWAIT
JORDAN
IRAQ
IRAN
AFGHANISTAN
PAKISTAN
INDIA
NEPAL BHUTAN
BANGLADESH
BURMA
ARABIAN
SEA
BAY OF
BENGAL
SRI
LANKA
MALDIVES
ANDAMAN
ISLANDS
(INDIA)
NICOBAR
ISLANDS
(INDIA)
THAILAND
VIETNAM
LAOS
CAMBODIA
SOUTH
CHINA
SEA
PHILIPPINE
SEA
TAIWAN
PHILIPPINES
GUAM
(U.S.A.)
NORTHERN
MARIANA ISLANDS
(U.S.A.)
MARSHALL
ISLANDS
(U.S.A.)
PALAU
MICRONESIA
BRUNEI
SINGAPORE
MALAYSIA
NAURU

INDONESIA

SEYCHELLES

INDIAN

OCEAN

COMOROS

MADAGASCAR

ANGOLA
ZAMBIA
ZIMBABWE
NAMIBIA
BOTSWANA
MOZAMBIQUE
MALAWI
SWAZILAND
LESOTHO
SOUTH
AFRICA

MAURITIUS

REUNION
(FRANCE)

COCOS ISLANDS
(AUSTRALIA)

CHRISTMAS
ISLAND
(AUSTRALIA)

PAPUA
NEW GUINEA

SOLOMON
ISLANDS

VANUATU

NEW CALEDONIA
(FRANCE)

AUSTRALIA

NEW
ZEALAND

CHATHAM
ISLANDS
(N.Z.)

KERGUELEN
(FRANCE)

Capital cities of the world
Every country has a main city, called
its capital. You can find a list of all the
countries of the world that are shown in
this atlas and the names of their capital
cities on pages 44 and 45.

CTICA

All about maps

Have you ever used a map to help you find your way somewhere? Picture maps show us where things are in a particular place. Usually a map is a flat drawing of an area or a place, called a plan view. There are many different types of maps that help people to travel around in our world.

Mapping a journey

You can find out more about how maps work by drawing one for yourself. The large map on this page shows Peter's journey to school.

Try drawing your own journey to school or to the local shops. To help you, imagine you are a bird looking down on your local area. Think about the things you would pass on your journey and then draw them on your map.

Journey line

Draw a coloured line on your map from your home to your journey's end. This will show the route that you take. Can you name the things that Peter passes on his way to school?

Map keys

Most maps use symbols of real things to give us information about a place. Each symbol is explained on the map in a list called a key.

Tree symbol

Peter's picture map uses this tree symbol to show areas where there are lots of trees.

Start of the journey
Start drawing a journey line at the place where your journey begins.

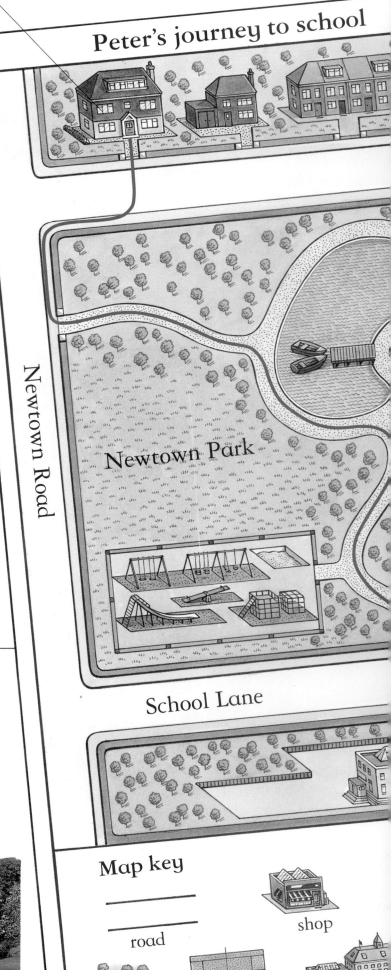

Peter's journey to school

Newtown Road

Newtown Park

School Lane

Map key

road

shop

trees

tennis courts

school

Things you see

Draw the things that you see on your journey, such as a block of flats or some shops. These symbols can be included in your key.

Park Road

High Street

Road names

Write in the names of the roads shown on your picture map.

Map colours

Colour in your picture map to help show what things are.

Journey's end

Draw an arrow on the journey line to mark the place where your journey ends.

Map key

Draw a key to explain all of the symbols you use on your picture map.

block of flats

house

play area

grass

path

Types of map

Look at these different kinds of map. Who might need to get information from each of these maps? Do you know of any other types of map that people use?

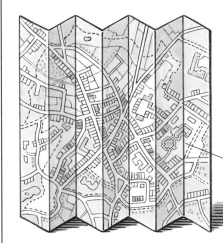

Town map
A town map names all the streets and important buildings in a town, such as the town hall or the railway station.

Town maps often fold out to make one large map.

Air routes map
This world map shows the major air routes for aeroplanes travelling to airports all over the world.

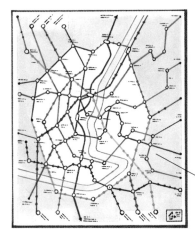

Underground map
An underground map shows a plan of the underground stations and railway tracks that cross a big city.

Underground maps are often printed on small, pocket-sized cards.

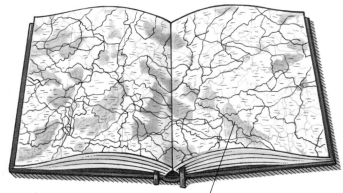

Road map
A road map shows all the roads that link one town to another and to the surrounding countryside.

Road maps are often collected in a book called a road atlas.

15

Using this atlas

Each map in this book looks at a different region of our world. The picture maps will help you to find out about each continent, its climate and terrain, and the people, plants, and animals that live there.

Map information

This map of West and South Asia is typical of the maps you will find in this book. Read the notes on this page to help you understand the information shown in the pictures on each map.

Locator globe
There is a world globe with every map. The red area on the globe shows where the countries on the map are situated on the Earth.

Natural resources
Drawings on the map show the natural resources, such as oil, that can be found in each region.

Climate and terrain
The climate, or usual weather, in each part of the world affects what the terrain (land) looks like and the people, animals, and plants that live there. The key below explains the types of climate and terrain shown in the maps in this book.

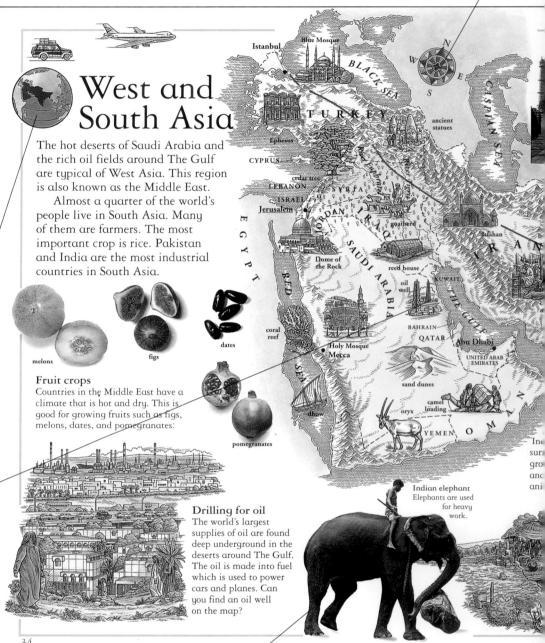

Compass
The compass needle on each map always points to the North Pole, so that you can see in which direction North, South, East, and West are.

West and South Asia

The hot deserts of Saudi Arabia and the rich oil fields around The Gulf are typical of West Asia. This region is also known as the Middle East.
  Almost a quarter of the world's people live in South Asia. Many of them are farmers. The most important crop is rice. Pakistan and India are the most industrial countries in South Asia.

Fruit crops
Countries in the Middle East have a climate that is hot and dry. This is good for growing fruits such as figs, melons, dates, and pomegranates.

Drilling for oil
The world's largest supplies of oil are found deep underground in the deserts around The Gulf. The oil is made into fuel which is used to power cars and planes. Can you find an oil well on the map?

Indian elephant
Elephants are used for heavy work.

34

Colourful photographs
Clear colour photographs show you details of the people, buildings, plants, and animals that are special to each region.

Grassland

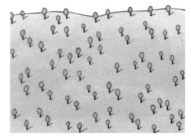

Grasslands are flat regions where grass and low bushes grow. Grasslands are home to many different animals.

Rainforest

Rainforests are hot, steamy forests that grow in very warm regions near the Equator, where it rains a lot.

Coniferous forest

Forests of conifer trees often grow in cold areas. These evergreen trees keep their leaves all year round.

Deciduous forest

Forests of deciduous trees grow in warmer places. Many deciduous trees lose their leaves in the autumn.

Journey box

The journey box follows the red journey line on each map from one city to another. It tells you how long the journey takes. If you compare the times of different journeys, you will know which continents are larger than others.

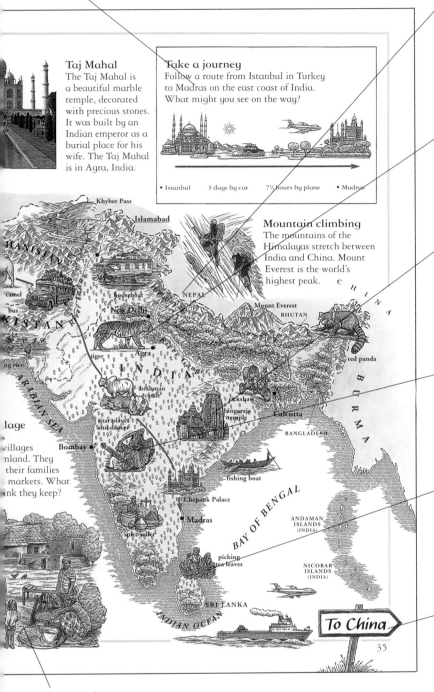

Taj Mahal
The Taj Mahal is a beautiful marble temple, decorated with precious stones. It was built by an Indian emperor as a burial place for his wife. The Taj Mahal is in Agra, India.

Take a journey
Follow a route from Istanbul in Turkey to Madras on the east coast of India. What might you see on the way?

• Istanbul   3 days by car   7½ hours by plane   • Madras

Mountain climbing
The mountains of the Himalayas stretch between India and China. Mount Everest is the world's highest peak.

Bordering countries
Areas shown in pale yellow are not part of the map. You can find out about these countries on another page.

Animals and plants
Drawings on the map show the animals and plants that live wild in each region.

Buildings
Drawings on the map show typical homes and famous buildings in each region.

Things people do
Drawings on the map show you how people spend their time in each region.

Crops and farming
Drawings on the map show what crops and animals people farm in each region.

Where next?
The signpost at the end of each map tells you in which country you will start the journey on the next page.

Artwork scenes
Detailed scenes of people and places show you more about how people live and work in one of the areas shown on the map.

Snow and ice

Some lands are frozen with ice and snow all year long. If the ice melts in summer, then moss and lichen can grow.

Desert
Deserts are very hot or cold areas with little fresh water. Few animals or plants can survive here.

Mountains
Mountains are high areas of rocky land. Their peaks are often very cold and may be covered with snow.

Map key
This key shows you the symbols used on each map and what they mean.

I N D I A	The name of a country
	The border between countries
	The border between states or provinces
Bombay •	A city
New Delhi •	A capital city
Lake Victoria	A lake
River Congo	A river
ARABIAN SEA	Seas and oceans
	A mountain **Kamchatka volcano**
	Animals and plants **Bactrian camel**
	Famous places **Dome of the Rock**
	Things people do **growing rice**

Antarctica

Antarctica is the coldest continent on Earth. This land of thick ice and snow surrounds the South Pole. The only creatures that can survive on the icy land are tiny insects. During the summer months, the ice around the edges melts. Penguins and other animals live in the sea and nest on nearby islands.

Take a journey
Follow a journey from Halley Station to Dumont d'Urville Station. There would be nothing to see but ice and snow.

• Halley Station	2 days by car	5 hours by plane	• Dumont d'Urville Station

Research station
The only people who live in Antarctica are scientists. They live in research stations and travel on sledges with motors, called snowmobiles. Can you find a station on the map?

Dressed for the cold
Scientists wear special clothes to keep their bodies warm in the freezing cold weather. They come to study the wildlife and learn about the rocks and the weather in this frozen area.

cruise ship

leopard seal

South Polar skua

Halley Station

Antarctic cod

ATLANTIC OCEAN

snow petrels

emperor penguins

ANTARCTICA

Amundsen-Scott Station

SOUTH POLE

Transantarctic Mountains

krill

PACIFIC OCEAN

ROSS ICE SHELF

Vostok

elephant seal

chinstrap penguins

blue whale

Dumont d'Urville Station

INDIAN OCEAN

humpback whale

To the Arctic

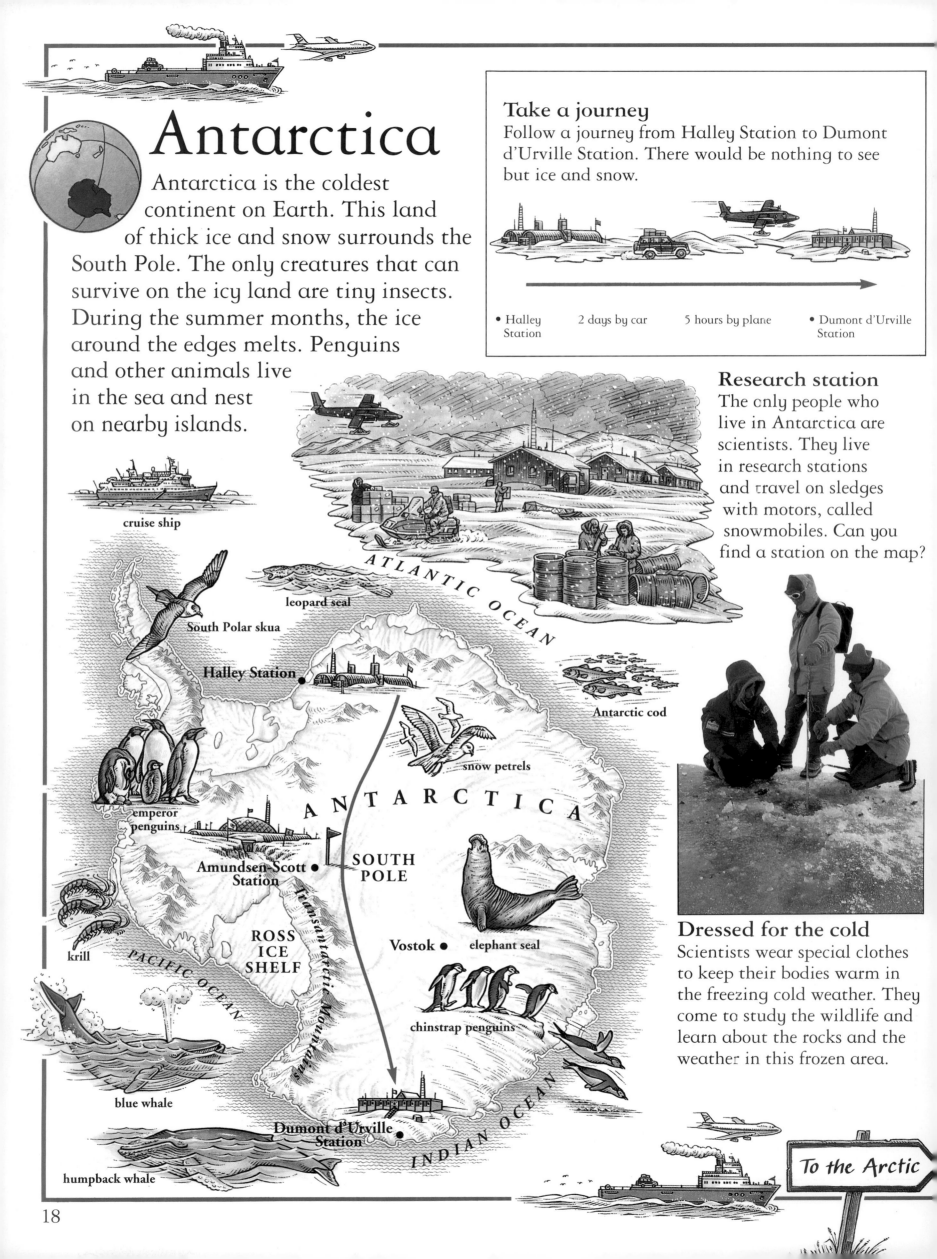

The Arctic

The most northern part of the Earth is the North Pole. The frozen sea and islands that surround it are called the Arctic. It is so cold here that the Arctic Ocean is frozen for most of the year. Unlike Antarctica, there are many kinds of animals and plants that live here.

Polar bear
The polar bear has a thick coat of white fur to keep it warm.

Greenland
Greenland is the world's largest island. The town of Nuuk is the country's capital. Here the main industry is fishing for cod and shrimp.

RUSSIAN FEDERATION

grey whales

long-tailed skua

walrus

ARCTIC OCEAN

elk

dog team and snowmobiles

snow goose

CANADA

DEVON ISLAND

ELLESMERE ISLAND

NORTH POLE

hooded seal

musk ox

GREENLAND (DENMARK)

SVALBARD (NORWAY)

ptarmigan

killer whale

Nuuk

lemmings

cod

fishing boat

narwhal

Take a journey
Follow a journey across the Arctic from the North Pole to Nuuk in Greenland. How many different animals might you see on the journey?

- North Pole   2 days by car   5 hours by plane   • Nuuk

Icebergs
Huge blocks of ice that break away from the frozen sea are called icebergs. These are a danger to ships because only a small part of an iceberg shows above the water. Most of it is hidden under the sea.

To Canada

19

Canada and Alaska

Canada and Alaska cover the northern half of North America. Canada is the second largest country in the world. However, not many people live there. This is because much of the north of Canada is covered in forests and lakes and is frozen for most of the year. Alaska, which lies to the northwest of Canada, is the largest state in the United States of America. Great supplies of oil have been found there.

Cutting down trees
Many of the pine trees that grow in Canada are cut down and sawn into logs. The logs of wood, called timber, are used to build houses and to make furniture.

Icebreaker ship
This powerful ship is used to break up the thick blocks of ice that form in the cold Arctic Ocean. Can you find the Arctic Ocean on the map?

Growing wheat
In Canada, wheat is grown on vast areas of flat land called the prairies. Wheat is used to make flour for baking into bread. Can you see any wheat fields on the map?

Combine harvester
This giant machine is used to cut and collect the wheat.

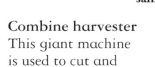

polar bear

Arctic hare

BANKS ISLAND

musk ox

VICTORIA ISLAND

Arctic fox

Yukon River

ALASKA (U.S.A.)

grizzly bear

Mount McKinley

YUKON TERRITORY

Yellowkn

Mackenzie River

Rocky Mountains

timber

walruses

oil tanker

salmon

BRITISH COLUMBIA

moose

ALBER

Fraser River

PACIFIC OCEAN

Vancouver

UNITED

BERING SEA

The first Canadians
The first people to live in northern Canada were the Inuit. This Inuit village is on Baffin Island.

Take a journey
The country of Canada is divided into 10 provinces and two northern territories. Follow a route from Vancouver to Ottawa. How many provinces would you pass through on the way?

• Vancouver $2\frac{1}{4}$ days by car $5\frac{1}{2}$ hours by plane   • Ottawa

Whale watching
People go to watch humpback whales playing in the sea around the coast of Newfoundland. In the cold winter months, they swim south to where the sea is warmer. What other animals live around the coasts of Canada?

OCEAN

ELLESMERE ISLAND

GREENLAND (DENMARK)

Baffin Bay

QUEEN ELIZABETH ISLANDS

BAFFIN ISLAND

ringed seal

Inuit hunters

hooded seal

NORTHWEST TERRITORIES

caribou

Canada goose

NEWFOUNDLAND

beluga whales

black bear

gannet

N

Hudson Bay

QUEBEC

PRINCE EDWARD ISLAND

porpoises

A

MANITOBA

NEW BRUNSWICK

NOVA SCOTIA

ATLANTIC OCEAN

ce hockey

D

maple trees

beaver

A

KATCHEWAN

Lake Winnipeg

ONTARIO

Parliament buildings

Ottawa

Winnipeg

Lake Ontario

wheat fields

Lake Superior

Lake Michigan

Toronto

Lake Huron

Niagara Falls

To the U.S.A.

TES OF AMERICA

Lake Erie

United States of America

The United States of America (U.S.A.) is one of the largest countries in the world. It has deserts, mountains, forests, and a vast area of flat land called the Great Plains. Part of North America, the country is made up of 50 states, each with its own capital city. The state of Alaska, shown on page 20, lies to the northwest of Canada.

San Francisco
The city of San Francisco is on the west coast of the U.S.A. The city is built on several hills and people ride on cable-cars that climb the steep streets. Some buildings are designed to survive the earthquakes that happen here.

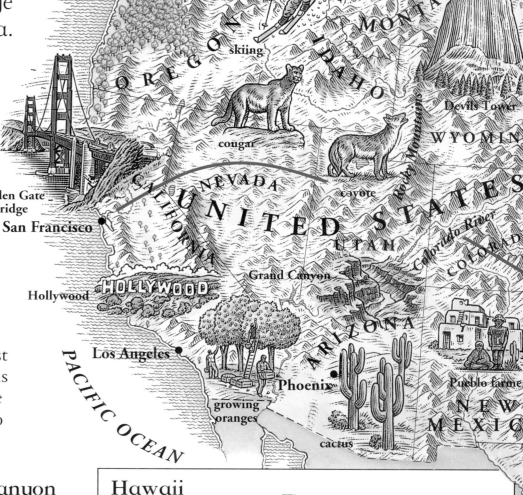

CANADA

WASHINGTON

salmon

harvesting wheat

OREGON

skiing

MONTANA

IDAHO

cougar

Devils Tower

WYOMING

coyote

NEVADA

UNITED STATES

CALIFORNIA

Golden Gate Bridge

San Francisco

UTAH

Colorado River

COLORADO

HOLLYWOOD

Grand Canyon

Hollywood

ARIZONA

Los Angeles

Phoenix

cactus

growing oranges

Pueblo farmer

NEW MEXICO

PACIFIC OCEAN

Grand Canyon
The Grand Canyon is a deep river valley in Arizona. The canyon was formed by the Colorado River cutting through the Rocky Mountains. Can you find the Grand Canyon on the map?

Hawaii
The 50th state of the U.S.A. is a group of islands in the Pacific called Hawaii. Visitors come to surf in the Pacific Ocean and to see the volcanoes.

KAUAI

MOLOKAI

OAHU

MAUI

HAWAII

surfer

Kilauea volcano

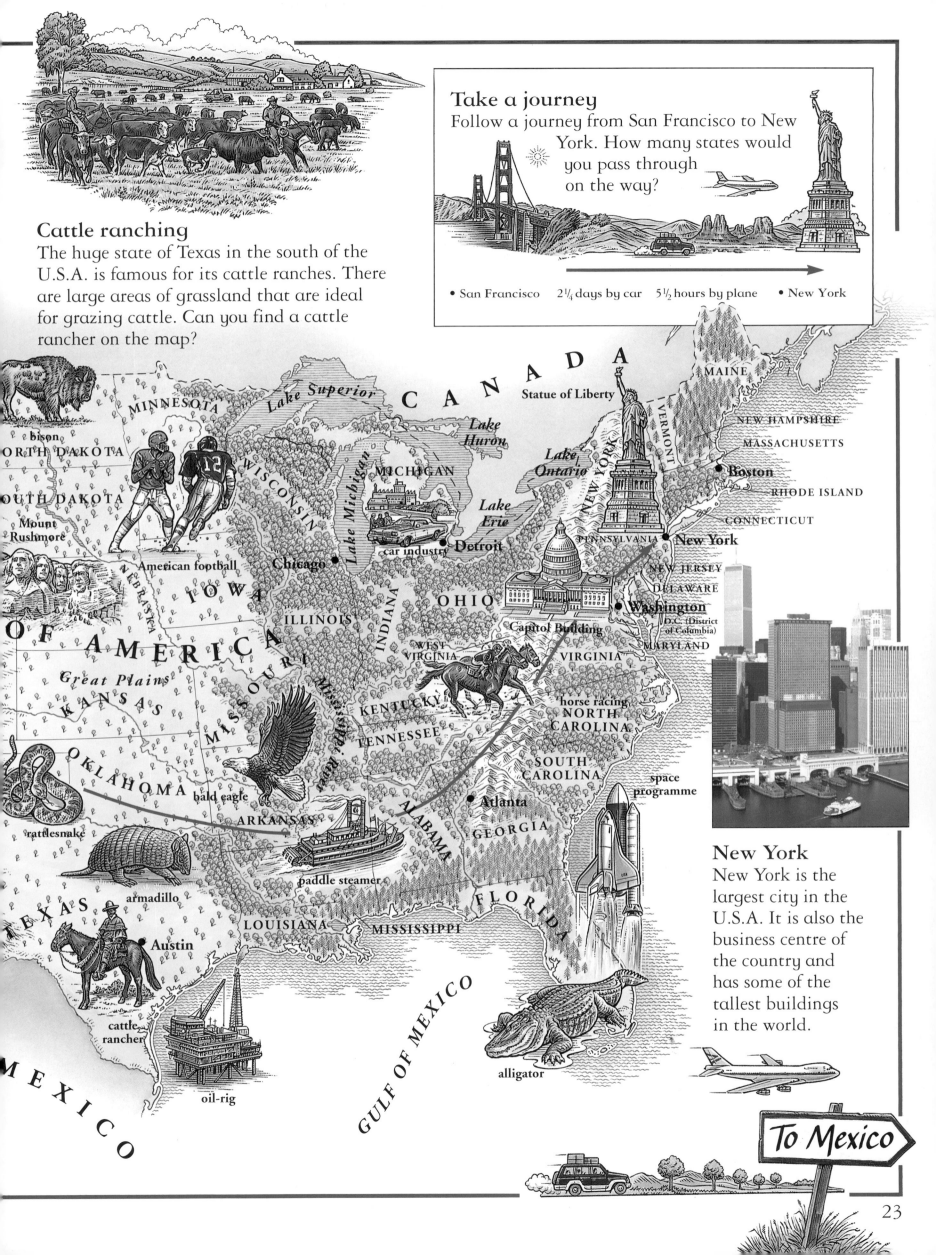

Cattle ranching

The huge state of Texas in the south of the U.S.A. is famous for its cattle ranches. There are large areas of grassland that are ideal for grazing cattle. Can you find a cattle rancher on the map?

Take a journey

Follow a journey from San Francisco to New York. How many states would you pass through on the way?

• San Francisco   2¼ days by car   5½ hours by plane   • New York

New York

New York is the largest city in the U.S.A. It is also the business centre of the country and has some of the tallest buildings in the world.

CANADA

MINNESOTA

Lake Superior

Statue of Liberty

MAINE

VERMONT

NEW HAMPSHIRE

MASSACHUSETTS

bison

NORTH DAKOTA

WISCONSIN

Lake Huron

Lake Ontario

NEW YORK

• Boston

RHODE ISLAND

SOUTH DAKOTA

MICHIGAN

Lake Erie

CONNECTICUT

Mount Rushmore

Lake Michigan

car industry

• Detroit

PENNSYLVANIA

• New York

American football

Chicago •

NEBRASKA

IOWA

ILLINOIS

INDIANA

OHIO

Capitol Building

Washington D.C. (District of Columbia)

NEW JERSEY

DELAWARE

MARYLAND

OF AMERICA

Great Plains

KANSAS

MISSOURI

WEST VIRGINIA

VIRGINIA

horse racing

NORTH CAROLINA

rattlesnake

OKLAHOMA

bald eagle

KENTUCKY

TENNESSEE

SOUTH CAROLINA

space programme

Mississippi River

ARKANSAS

paddle steamer

ALABAMA

• Atlanta

GEORGIA

armadillo

TEXAS

• Austin

cattle rancher

LOUISIANA

MISSISSIPPI

FLORIDA

oil-rig

MEXICO

GULF OF MEXICO

alligator

To Mexico

Central and South America

Central America is a narrow strip of land that joins North America and South America. The country of Panama has a canal that allows ships to sail from the Atlantic to the Pacific Ocean. Much of South America is rainforest, mountains, or grasslands called pampas. Farmers make money by growing bananas, sugar cane, and coffee. The world's longest chain of mountains, called the Andes, runs down the west coast of South America.

West Indies

In the Caribbean Sea, there are hundreds of large and small islands. These are the West Indies. The sea is usually calm, but the islands sometimes have storms known as hurricanes.

BAHAMAS

CUBA

coconut trees

CAYMAN ISLANDS (U.K.)

JAMAICA

HAITI

DOMINICAN REPUBLIC

PUERTO RICO (U.S.A.)

GUADELOUPE (FRANCE)

ST LUCIA

BARBADOS

GRENADA

TRINIDAD AND TOBAGO

cruise ship

CARIBBEAN SEA

coral reef

Grenada has beautiful beaches.

Buenos Aires

The capital of Argentina is Buenos Aires. It is one of the largest cities in South America and a major port. What products do you think are shipped from here?

Football

Football is a favourite sport in South America. It is played everywhere, even on beaches and in the streets of towns.

N
E
S
W

UNITED STATES OF AMERICA

MEXICO

Mexico City

prickly pear

Gila monster

GULF OF MEXICO

Chichén Itzá

green turtle

growing avocados

GUATEMALA

BELIZE

HONDURAS

EL SALVADOR

NICARAGUA

toucan

COSTA RICA

Panama Canal

PACIFIC OCEAN

Angel Falls

ATLANTIC OCEAN

GUIANA (FRANCE)

capybara

BRAZIL

Brazil nuts

growing bananas

cutting sugar cane

Rio de Janeiro

growing cocoa

picking coffee

River Amazon

Amazonian Indian

jaguar

PERU

condor

market scene

Andes Mountains

BOLIVIA

Machu Picchu

ATACAMA DESERT

reed boat

CHILE

PARAGUAY

gaucho cattle herder

anteater

URUGUAY

Buenos Aires

ARGENTINA

ATLANTIC OCEAN

Andes Mountains

sheep

penguins

fur seals

Tierra del Fuego

FALKLAND ISLANDS (U.K.)

To the U.K.

Llamas
Llamas are used to carry goods along narrow mountain roads.

The Amazon rainforest
The River Amazon flows through a huge rainforest. Rainforests grow in countries that are hot and have a lot of rain. Many kinds of birds, animals, and plants live there.

Ancient city
The ruins of a very old city can be seen in Machu Picchu, Peru. These ruins tell us about the Incas, the people who lived there hundreds of years ago. Can you find Machu Picchu on the map?

The people of Peru
Many of the people of Peru live in villages in the mountains of the Andes. The farmers grow maize, potatoes, and beans. The women use animal hair to weave colourful cloth, which they sell in local markets.

Take a journey
Follow a journey from Mexico City in Mexico to Rio de Janeiro in Brazil. How many countries would you pass through on the way?

• Mexico City   4 days by car   10 hours by plane   • Rio de Janeiro

25

North Europe

The countries of Denmark, Norway, and Sweden make up the area called Scandinavia. Finland also borders the Baltic Sea and Iceland lies in the Atlantic Ocean. Much of the land has lakes, forests, and mountains and is covered with snow during the winter months. The United Kingdom (U.K.) is made up of England, Northern Ireland, Scotland, and Wales. Europe has many important natural resources, such as oil and gas from the North Sea, timber from the forests, and fish in the surrounding seas.

Iceland

Iceland is often called the land of ice and fire. This cold and windy island is covered with huge sheets of ice and there are also many volcanoes. Fountains of hot water, called geysers, are forced out of the ground.

Reykjavik — volcano — ICELAND — ice sheet — geyser — fishing boat

London

London is the capital city of the United Kingdom. The British government makes laws in the Houses of Parliament. These buildings form the Palace of Westminster, which has a famous clock tower known as Big Ben.

Big Ben

Take a journey

Follow a route from Plymouth in England to Edinburgh in Scotland. What might you see on the way?

• Plymouth   10 hours by car   1 hour by plane   • Edinburgh

FAEROE ISLANDS (DENMARK)

ATLANTIC OCEAN

oil and natural gas

mackerel

SCOTLAND

Edinburgh Castle

Edinburgh

NORTHERN IRELAND

UNITED KINGDOM

• Belfast

REPUBLIC OF IRELAND

• Dublin

sheep

digging peat

WALES

ENGLAND

cricket

Cardiff

• London

lighthouse

Plymouth

ENGLISH CHANNEL

FRANCE

NORTH

ARCTIC OCEAN

Coast of Norway

The coast of Norway has lots of inlets with steep sides. These are called fjords. They were made thousands of years ago by ice cutting into the land.

• Tromso

Sami family

lynx

eagle

wolf

NORWAY

SWEDEN

FINLAND

GULF OF BOTHNIA

paper mill

hydroelectric power

seals

Bergen

• Oslo

Helsinki

Tallinn

saw mill

stave church

Lake Vanern

Stockholm

ESTONIA

BALTIC SEA

glass blower

SKAGERRAK

KATTEGAT

Riga

LATVIA

houses in Riga

pig farming

LITHUANIA

DENMARK

Copenhagen

fishing boat

Vilnius

EA

POLAND

Reindeer

The reindeer is a kind of large deer that lives in cold regions. The Sami people keep large herds of reindeer and use their fur to make clothes. Can you find the Sami people on the map?

Timber industry

Pine and fir trees grow in the cold forests of Sweden, Norway, and Finland. They provide wood, which is used to make paper for books and newspapers.

Pine cones
Pine trees grow their seeds in hard, wooden cones.

Take a journey

Follow a route from Tromso in Norway to Riga in Latvia. How many countries would you pass through on your journey?

| • Tromso | 1 day by car | 2¼ hours by plane | • Riga |

To the Netherlands

Central Europe

Many of the countries in Central Europe are fairly flat. Most of the main cities and industries are in the north. Further east, in Poland and Hungary, the land is used for farming and coal-mining. Several long rivers run through Europe. They are used to transport goods from one place to another. In the south, there are high, snow-capped mountains called the Alps. The Alps stretch from France through Italy, Switzerland, and Austria.

NORTH SEA

canal boat

making sausages

storks

Amsterdam

Berlin

NETHERLANDS

Brandenburg Gate

Brussels

BELGIUM

making chocolates

making cars

Luxembourg

LUXEMBOURG

Frankfurt

red deer

GERMANY

River Rhine

Neuschwanstein Castle

Munich

N
W   E
S

FRANCE

SWITZERLAND

Alps

AUSTRIA

Berne

LIECHTENSTEIN

ITALY

Matterhorn

Alpine flowers
High up in the mountains, small flowers grow between the rocks or low on the ground. This keeps them out of the cold winds.

Blue gentian

St. John's ragwort

The Alps
The scenery in the Alps is very pretty. There are forests, lakes, and rivers. Many people visit the mountains for skiing holidays. Special lifts take them up to the snow. Can you find any other mountains on the map?

BALTIC SEA

RUSSIAN FEDERATION

LITHUANIA

BELORUSSIA

Gdansk

wooden windmill

P O L A N D

European bison

Oder

coal-mining

River Elbe

Warsaw

River Vistula

growing sugar beet

sheep

UKRAINE

● **Prague**

CZECH REPUBLIC

Church of Our Lady before Tyn

Carpathian Mountains

SLOVAKIA

ROMANIA

Vienna

Alps

Lipizzaner horse

● **Bratislava**

River Danube

● **Budapest**

Parliament building

street market

SLOVENIA   CROATIA

H U N G A R Y

YUGOSLAVIA

Ship-building

Ship-building is an important industry in Poland. Ships are made from steel. Coal and iron are mined in Poland and used to make the steel. There are ports for ships on the coast of the Baltic Sea. Can you find the port of Gdansk on the map?

Windmill
A windmill is powered by the wind, which turns four large sails. Can you find a windmill on the map?

Dutch tulips
The flat fields in the Netherlands are used for farming. Many Dutch farmers grow flowers, such as tulips. Windmills pump water into the fields.

To Portugal

Take a journey
Follow a route from Amsterdam in the Netherlands to Budapest in Hungary. What might you see in the different countries on the way?

| ● Amsterdam | 20 hours by car | 2 hours by plane | ● Budapest |

South Europe

The southern countries of Europe have many historical cities with famous buildings to visit. They also have important industries such as steelworks and car-making. These countries have hot, dry summers. The weather is good for growing oranges, tomatoes, and olives. Grapes are grown in many countries, such as France, and are used to make wine.

Along the coast
Most countries in South Europe have a coastline. Many people in Spain and Portugal make their living by fishing. Tourists also come to enjoy the sunny beaches. Can you find any tourists on the Greek island of Crete?

Water sports
In the warm Mediterranean Sea, water sports such as windsurfing and sailing are very popular. People like to sail along the coast and around the islands.

UNITED KINGDOM

ENGLISH CHANNEL

Eiffel Tower

Paris

FRANCE

vineyard

BAY OF BISCAY

Camargue horses

N
W   E
S

brown bear

Bilbao

River Ebro

ANDORRA

Royal Palace

Barcelona

PORTUGAL

Belem Tower

Lisbon

Madrid

S P A I N

yacht

MINOR

MAJORCA

flamenco dancers

Valencia

IBIZA

Seville

picking oranges

MEDITERRANEA

lobster

Take a journey
Follow a route across Europe, from Lisbon in Portugal to Athens in Greece. How many countries would you pass through on the way?

• Lisbon   2¼ days by car   5½ hours by plane   • Athens

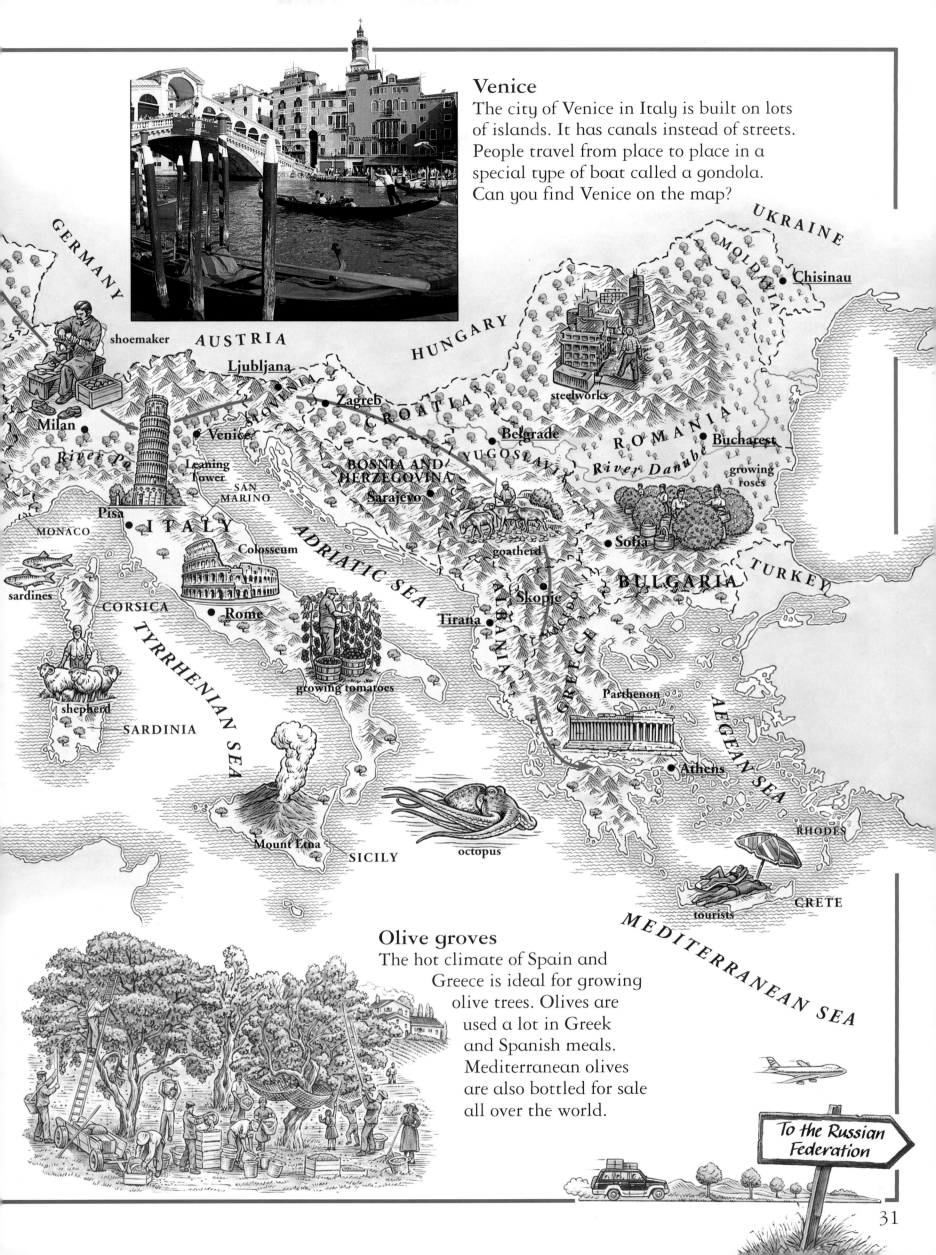

Venice

The city of Venice in Italy is built on lots of islands. It has canals instead of streets. People travel from place to place in a special type of boat called a gondola. Can you find Venice on the map?

UKRAINE

GERMANY

MOLDAVIA

Chisinau

shoemaker

AUSTRIA

HUNGARY

steelworks

Ljubljana

Milan

SLOVENIA

Zagreb

River Po

Venice

CROATIA

Belgrade

ROMANIA

Bucharest

Leaning Tower

SAN MARINO

BOSNIA AND HERZEGOVINA

YUGOSLAVIA

River Danube

growing roses

Pisa

ITALY

Sarajevo

goatherd

MONACO

Colosseum

ADRIATIC SEA

Sofia

BULGARIA

TURKEY

sardines

CORSICA

Rome

Skopje

Tirana

MACEDONIA

ALBANIA

GREECE

Parthenon

AEGEAN SEA

shepherd

TYRRHENIAN SEA

growing tomatoes

SARDINIA

Athens

RHODES

Mount Etna

SICILY

octopus

CRETE

tourists

MEDITERRANEAN SEA

Olive groves

The hot climate of Spain and Greece is ideal for growing olive trees. Olives are used a lot in Greek and Spanish meals. Mediterranean olives are also bottled for sale all over the world.

To the Russian Federation

North Eurasia

North Eurasia includes part of Europe and part of Asia. There are 11 countries here including the Russian Federation, which is the largest country in the world. Much of the land is covered with forests, mountains, and lakes. In the northern region of Siberia, the weather is very cold. The southwest is much warmer. Oil, coal, and timber are found in North Eurasia.

RUSSIAN FEDERATION

Winter Palace

Murmansk

BELORUSSIA

St Petersburg

tractor factory

Kiev

Moscow

BLACK SEA

UKRAINE

River Don

River Volga

Ural Mountains

ballet dancers

tourists

GEORGIA
ARMENIA

timber barge

RUSSIA

AZERBAIJAN

CASPIAN SEA

IRAN

Kara Kum Desert

ARAL SEA

Astana

KAZAKHSTAN

Kyzyl Kum Desert

space centre

TURKMENISTAN

UZBEKISTAN

Ashgabat

Tashkent

AFGHANISTAN

KYRGYZSTAN

CHINA

TAJIKISTAN

Moscow
Many tourists come to visit the buildings in Moscow. St Basil's Cathedral is famous for its towers with coloured domes. Can you find Moscow on the map?

Growing crops
Farming is important in North Eurasia. The long, cold winters and lack of rain make farming difficult. Wheat, barley, sugar beet, and potatoes are the main crops. In the warmer south, farmers grow grapes, tea, and fruits such as melons.

ice-breaker ship

FRANZ JOSEF LAND

Coal fields
There are large coal fields in the Ukraine, Kazakhstan, and east Siberia. Much of the coal is used to supply power stations or to provide fuel for factories. What types of factory can you find on this map?

BERING STRAIT

NOVAYA ZEMLYA

SEVERNAYA ZEMLYA

ARCTIC OCEAN

grey whales

NEW SIBERIAN ISLANDS

River Kolyma

BERING SEA

wooden house (dacha)

reindeer herder

paper factory

Siberian leopard

Kamchatka volcano

oil-rigs

FEDERATION

SIBERIA

River Lena

fishing boat

packing fish

Lake Baikal

Irkutsk

Altai Mountains

MONGOLIA

Trans-Siberian Railway

CHINA

KURILE ISLANDS

Vladivostok

Take a journey
Follow a route across the Russian Federation from St Petersburg to Vladivostok. What might you see on the way?

• St Petersburg   4$\frac{1}{3}$ days by car   10$\frac{1}{2}$ hours by plane   • Vladivostok

To Turkey

West and South Asia

The hot deserts of Saudi Arabia and the rich oil fields around The Gulf are typical of West Asia. This region is also known as the Middle East.

Almost a quarter of the world's people live in South Asia. Many of them are farmers. The most important crop is rice. Pakistan and India are the most industrial countries in South Asia.

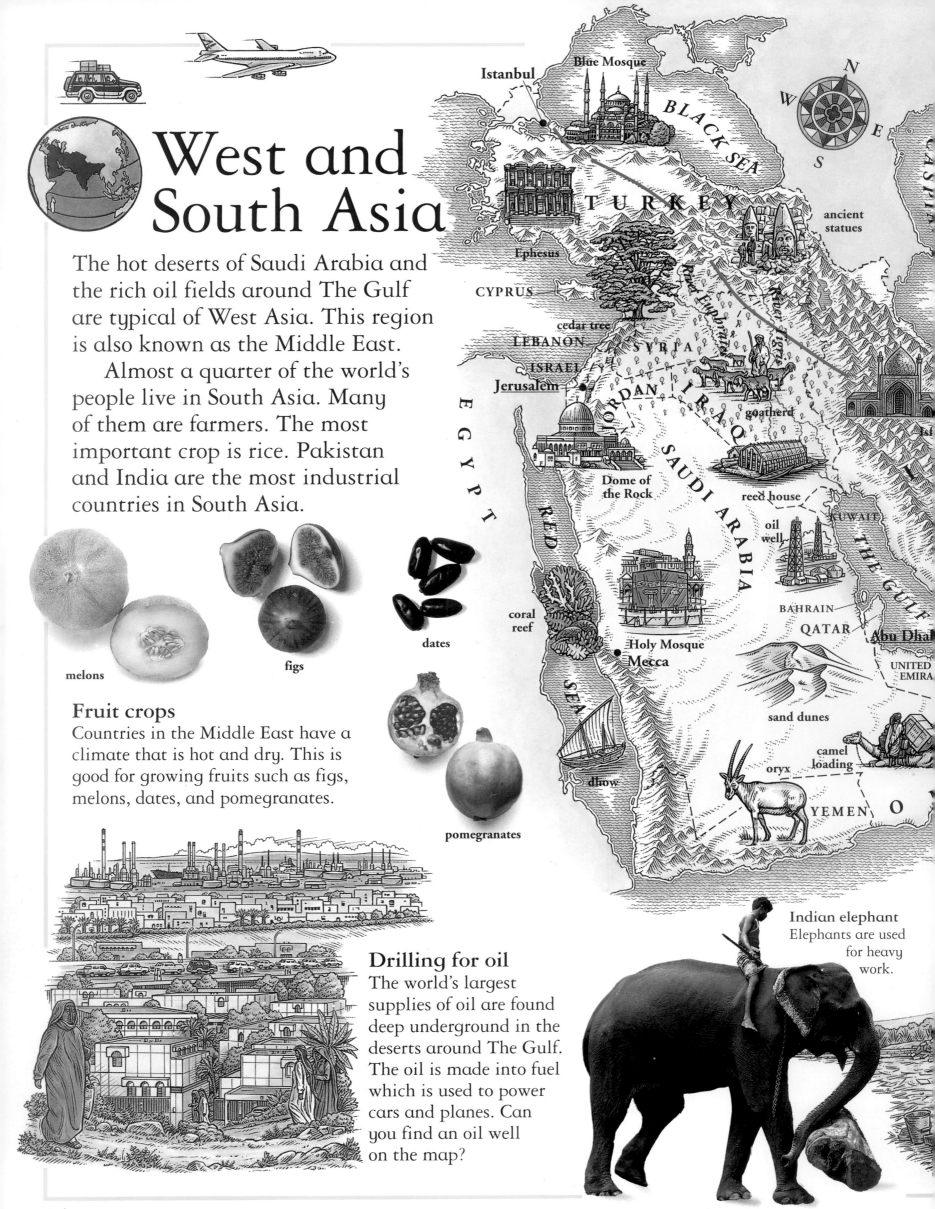

melons

figs

dates

Fruit crops
Countries in the Middle East have a climate that is hot and dry. This is good for growing fruits such as figs, melons, dates, and pomegranates.

pomegranates

Drilling for oil
The world's largest supplies of oil are found deep underground in the deserts around The Gulf. The oil is made into fuel which is used to power cars and planes. Can you find an oil well on the map?

Indian elephant
Elephants are used for heavy work.

Map labels
Istanbul
Blue Mosque
BLACK SEA
TURKEY
Ephesus
ancient statues
CYPRUS
cedar tree
LEBANON
SYRIA
River Euphrates
River Tigris
ISRAEL
JORDAN
IRAQ
Jerusalem
goatherd
Dome of the Rock
SAUDI ARABIA
reed house
oil well
KUWAIT
RED SEA
coral reef
BAHRAIN
QATAR
Abu Dhabi
Holy Mosque Mecca
UNITED EMIRA...
sand dunes
camel loading
THE GULF
dhow
oryx
YEMEN
O...

Taj Mahal
The Taj Mahal is a beautiful marble tomb, decorated with precious stones. It was built by an Indian emperor as a burial place for his wife. The Taj Mahal is in Agra, India.

Take a journey
Follow a route from Istanbul in Turkey to Madras on the east coast of India. What might you see on the way?

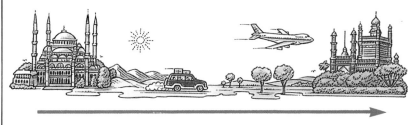

• Istanbul   3 days by car   7½ hours by plane   • Madras

Khyber Pass

Islamabad

AFGHANISTAN

Bactrian camel

carpet making

bus

PAKISTAN

River Indus

houseboat

growing rice

oil tanker

ARABIAN SEA

New Delhi

tiger

Agra

INDIA

River Ganges

brahman cattle

sitar player and dancer

Bombay

NEPAL

Mountain climbing
The mountains of the Himalayas stretch between India and China. Mount Everest is the world's highest peak.

Mount Everest

BHUTAN

CHINA

red panda

BURMA

rickshaw

Lingaraja temple

Calcutta

BANGLADESH

fishing boat

Chepauk Palace

• Madras

spice seller

BAY OF BENGAL

ANDAMAN ISLANDS (INDIA)

NICOBAR ISLANDS (INDIA)

picking tea leaves

SRI LANKA

INDIAN OCEAN

Indian village
Many people in India still live in villages surrounded by farmland. They grow crops to feed their families and to sell at local markets. What animals do you think they keep?

To China

East Asia

The countries of East Asia cover a large part of the mainland as well as many islands. China is the largest country and has deserts and high mountains in the region of Tibet. Most people live in the east, where the land is good for growing tea, rice, and wheat. Further south, the countries are hotter. Farmers grow crops such as rubber trees, tobacco plants, and pineapples.

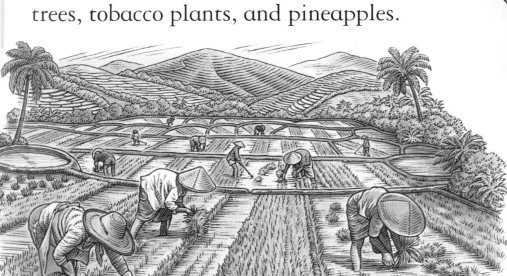

Rice growing

Rice is an important crop in countries such as Thailand and Malaysia. The hot climate and heavy rains during the monsoon are good for growing rice. Farmers use flat land and also cut fields into the steep hillsides. Can you find Thailand on the map?

Take a journey

Follow a route through China from Kashgar to Hong Kong. What interesting sights might you see on the way?

| • Kashgar | 3¼ days by car | 8 hours by plane | • Hong Kong |

RUSSIAN

MONGOLIA

mosque

Kashgar

Bactrian camel

Takla Makan Desert

Great Wall of China

K2 Mountain

TIBET

Chongqing

Himalayas

lammergeier

INDIA

terracotta army

BAY OF BENGAL

BURMA

LAOS

THAILAND

CAMBODIA

floating market

SUMATRA

SOUTH CHINA S

MA

SINGAP

rubber trees

Jakarta

IN

The streets of China

More people live in China than in any other country. Many people travel around the busy cities by bike.

FEDERATION

fossil hunting

tiger

~obi Desert

~low River

NORTH KOREA

Peking (Beijing)

Seoul

SOUTH KOREA

JAPAN

~icking tea leaves

River Yangtze

Shanghai

EAST CHINA SEA

~HINA

Hong Kong

TAIWAN

~AINAN

SOUTH CHINA SEA

PHILIPPINES

Manila

LUZON

~il tanker

MINDANAO

BRUNEI

~SIA

orang-utan

~RNEO

CELEBES

MOLUCCAS

~DONESIA

BANDA SEA

IRIAN JAYA INDONESIA

PAPUA NEW GUINEA

~AVA

TIMOR

BALI

AUSTRALIA

cranes

HOKKAIDO

HONSHU

JAPAN

Mount Fuji

Shinto temple

Tokyo

SHIKOKU

KYUSHU

loggerhead turtle

Japan

Japan is made up of hundreds of islands. The four main islands are Honshu, Hokkaido, Kyushu, and Shikoku. Mountains and woods cover much of the land. Most people live on the coasts or in big cities like Tokyo. On the island of Honshu there is a volcano named Mount Fuji. Can you find it on the map?

Tokyo

Tokyo is the capital city of Japan. Many people work in factories, which make cars, cameras, and electronic goods. The city also has beautiful gardens where people can walk and relax.

Fishing

Japanese people eat lots of fish. Japan catches more fish than any other country and has the world's biggest fleet of fishing boats.

Pandas

Giant pandas live in the cool mountains of central China. They feed on the bamboo plants that grow there. What other animals can you find in East Asia?

To Algeria

Africa

Africa is a huge, hot continent. It has the world's largest desert, the Sahara. Most Africans are farmers, and the food that they grow is sent all over the world. People also live and work in the crowded cities. There are many types of terrain in Africa, including deserts, grasslands, and rainforests. Many different birds and animals live here.

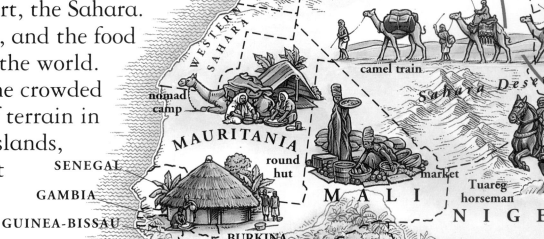

MOROCCO
Algiers
carpet seller
ALGERIA
TUNISIA
WESTERN SAHARA
camel train
Sahara Desert
nomad camp
MAURITANIA
round hut
MALI
market
Tuareg horseman
SENEGAL
GAMBIA
GUINEA-BISSAU
BURKINA
NIGER
GUINEA
River Niger
SIERRA LEONE
NIGERIA
LIBERIA
Lagos
IVORY COAST
GHANA
TOGO
BENIN
CAMEROON
container ship
EQUATORIAL GUINEA
ATLANTIC OCEAN
GABON
flying fish
CONGO
hornbill

Water in the desert
An oasis is a place in the desert where water is found. Can you find an oasis on the map?

Lovebird
The lovebird is one of many birds that live in the rainforest.

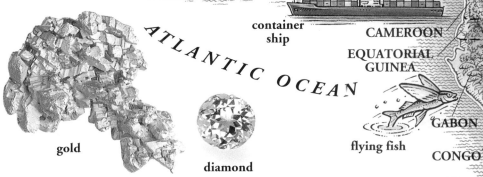

gold

diamond

Underground treasure
South Africa has many gold and diamond mines. Most of the diamonds used to make jewellery are found in South Africa.

Living by the river
In the rainforest, people build houses on stilts along the rivers where they live. Can you find the River Congo on the map?

Take a journey
Follow a route across Africa, from Algiers in Algeria to Cape Town in South Africa. What might you see on the way?

• Algiers   4 days by car   10 hours by plane   • Cape Town

Animals of the grasslands
Tourists come from all over the world to see the animals that live safely in Africa's nature reserves. Can you name some animals from the grasslands?

MEDITERRANEAN SEA

Suez Canal

Cairo

N
W E
S

pyramids

LIBYA

River Nile

SAUDI ARABIA

EGYPT

oasis

pelican

CHAD

crocodile

RED SEA

ostrich

ERITREA

hippopotamus

SUDAN

DJIBOUTI

crocodile

ETHIOPIA

Great Rift Valley

goatherds

CENTRAL AFRICAN REPUBLIC

gorilla

River Congo

UGANDA

KENYA

SOMALIA

CONGO (Zaire)

RWANDA
BURUNDI

Lake Victoria

Mount Kenya

INDIAN OCEAN

Mombasa

Kilimanjaro

elephants

masked dancer

TANZANIA

MALAWI

ANGOLA

ZAMBIA

River Zambezi

giraffe

zebra

ZIMBABWE

Victoria Falls

lemur

MOZAMBIQUE

MADAGASCAR

NAMIBIA

BOTSWANA

Ndebele house

chameleon

springbok

SWAZILAND

SOUTH AFRICA

LESOTHO

Cape Town

Lion
Lions hunt zebras and wildebeest that live in the hot grasslands.

Mombasa
Mombasa is a big, modern city on the coast of Kenya. Many thousands of people work in its factories, offices, and shops. The huge elephant tusks at the entrance to the city are made of metal.

To Australia

Australasia

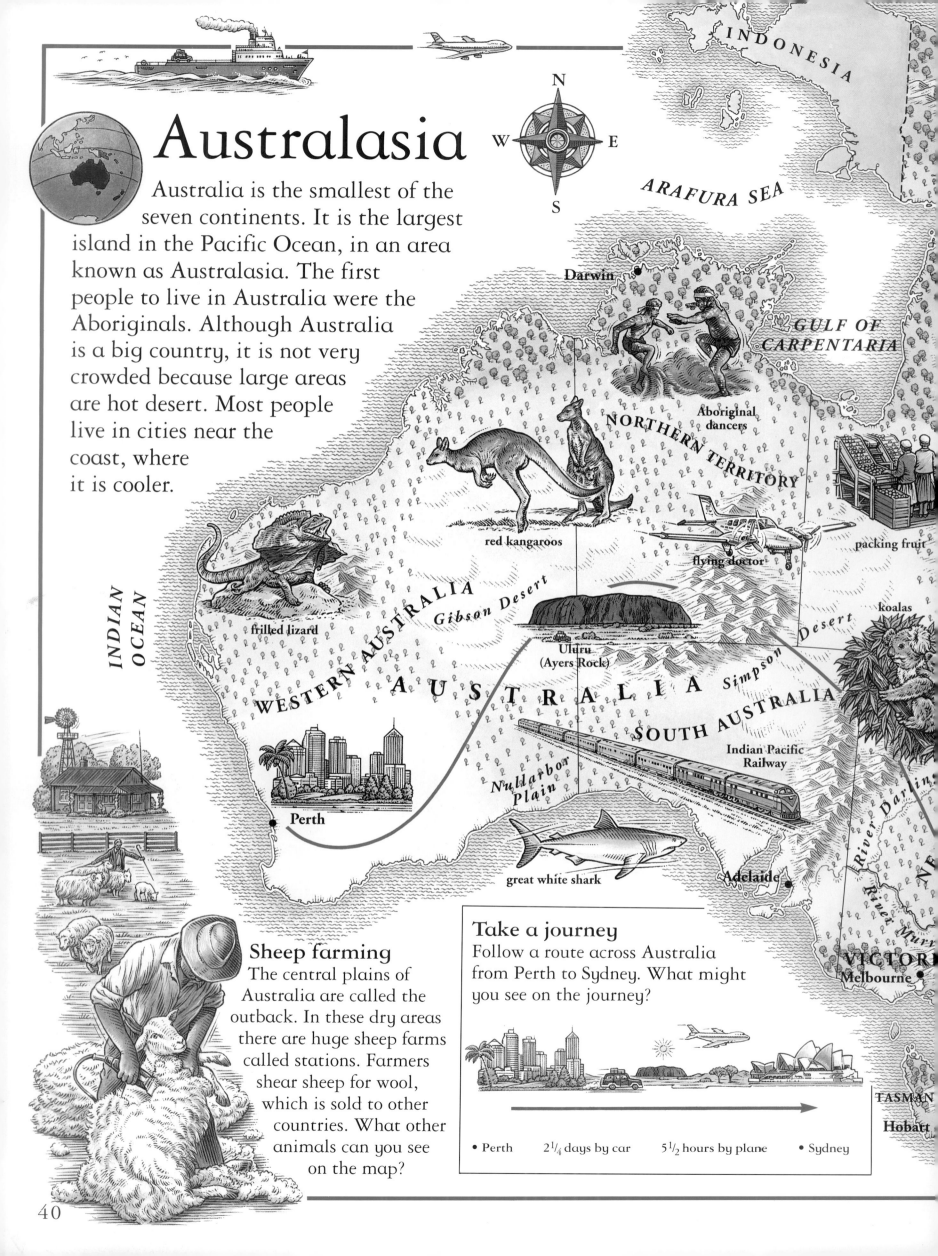

Australia is the smallest of the seven continents. It is the largest island in the Pacific Ocean, in an area known as Australasia. The first people to live in Australia were the Aboriginals. Although Australia is a big country, it is not very crowded because large areas are hot desert. Most people live in cities near the coast, where it is cooler.

INDONESIA

ARAFURA SEA

Darwin

GULF OF CARPENTARIA

Aboriginal dancers

NORTHERN TERRITORY

red kangaroos

flying doctor

packing fruit

koalas

INDIAN OCEAN

frilled lizard

WESTERN AUSTRALIA

Gibson Desert

A U S T R A L I A

Uluru (Ayers Rock)

Simpson

Desert

SOUTH AUSTRALIA

Indian Pacific Railway

Nullarbor Plain

Perth

great white shark

Adelaide

River Darling

River Murray

VICTORIA
Melbourne

TASMAN

Hobart

Sheep farming
The central plains of Australia are called the outback. In these dry areas there are huge sheep farms called stations. Farmers shear sheep for wool, which is sold to other countries. What other animals can you see on the map?

Take a journey
Follow a route across Australia from Perth to Sydney. What might you see on the journey?

• Perth   2¼ days by car   5½ hours by plane   • Sydney

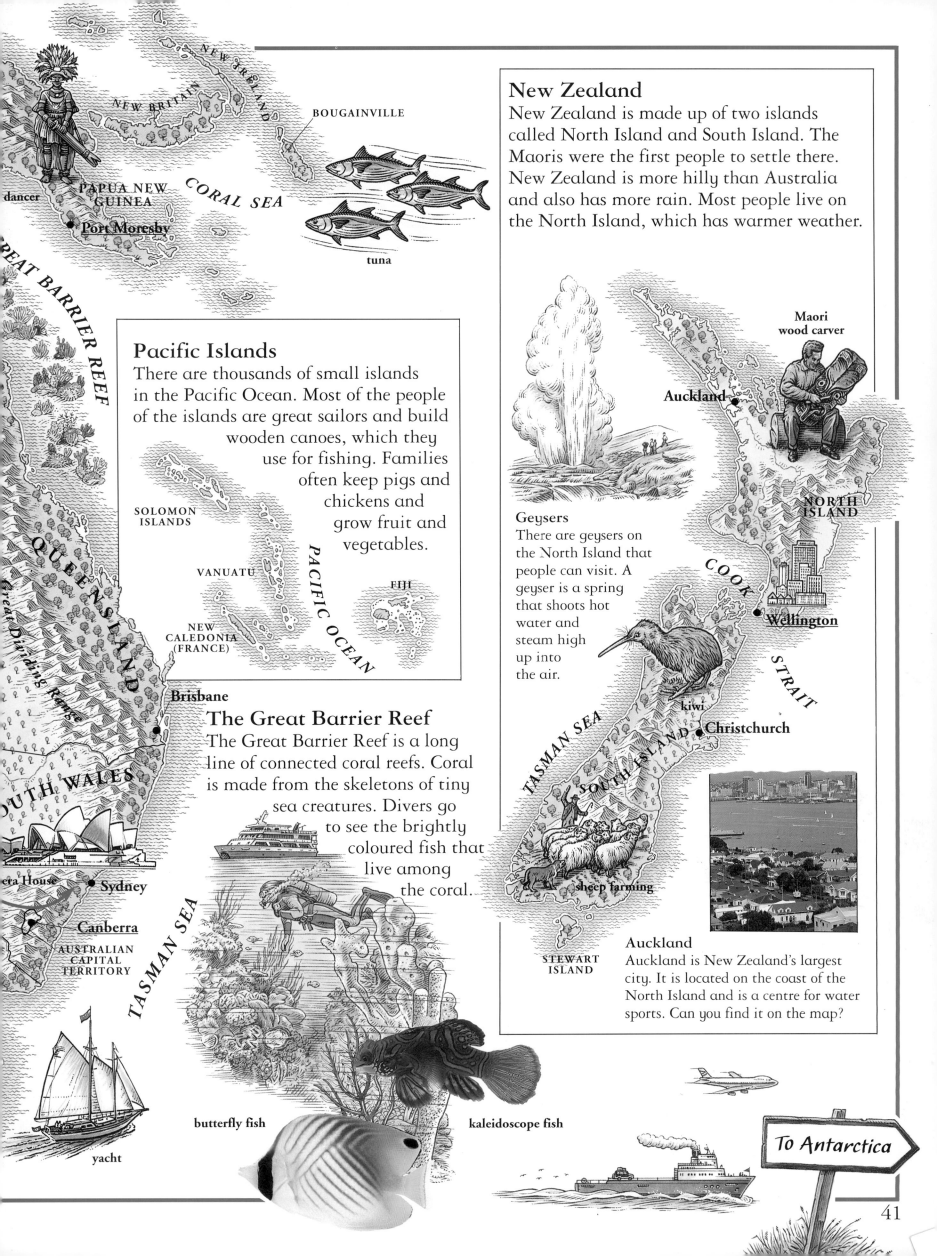

dancer

NEW IRELAND

NEW BRITAIN

BOUGAINVILLE

PAPUA NEW GUINEA

● Port Moresby

CORAL SEA

tuna

GREAT BARRIER REEF

QUEENSLAND

Great Dividing Range

Pacific Islands

There are thousands of small islands in the Pacific Ocean. Most of the people of the islands are great sailors and build wooden canoes, which they use for fishing. Families often keep pigs and chickens and grow fruit and vegetables.

SOLOMON ISLANDS

VANUATU

NEW CALEDONIA (FRANCE)

PACIFIC OCEAN

FIJI

Brisbane

The Great Barrier Reef

The Great Barrier Reef is a long line of connected coral reefs. Coral is made from the skeletons of tiny sea creatures. Divers go to see the brightly coloured fish that live among the coral.

OUTH WALES

era House

● Sydney

Canberra

AUSTRALIAN CAPITAL TERRITORY

TASMAN SEA

yacht

butterfly fish

kaleidoscope fish

New Zealand

New Zealand is made up of two islands called North Island and South Island. The Maoris were the first people to settle there. New Zealand is more hilly than Australia and also has more rain. Most people live on the North Island, which has warmer weather.

Maori wood carver

Auckland ●

NORTH ISLAND

Geysers

There are geysers on the North Island that people can visit. A geyser is a spring that shoots hot water and steam high up into the air.

COOK STRAIT

● Wellington

kiwi

● Christchurch

TASMAN SEA

SOUTH ISLAND

sheep farming

STEWART ISLAND

Auckland

Auckland is New Zealand's largest city. It is located on the coast of the North Island and is a centre for water sports. Can you find it on the map?

To Antarctica

41

Our amazing world

Here are some record-breaking facts and figures about some of the places in our amazing world. Can you find these places in your atlas?

Can you find these places in your atlas?

Did you know?

The Earth spins around at 1,600 km/h (1,000 mph).

The largest iceberg ever seen was floating off Antarctica. It was larger than the whole of Belgium.

The longest river is the River Nile in Africa. It is 6,670 km (4,145 miles) long.

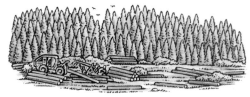

The largest forest covers part of the Russian Federation and Finland. It is larger than the whole of the U.S.A.

The largest ocean is the Pacific. It is larger than all of the land in the world put together.

Highest waterfall
979 m (3,212 ft)

Tallest geyser
457 m (1,499 ft)

Tallest building
452 m (1,488 ft)

  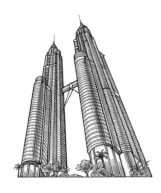

The Angel Falls in Venezuela are twice as high as the world's tallest building.

A geyser in New Zealand shot out water higher than the world's tallest building.

The tallest building is Petronas Towers in Kuala Lumpur, in Malaysia.

Most crowded city

More than 18 million people live in Mexico City – more people than live in the whole of Australia.

Most plants and animals

Over half of all plant and animal species live in the rainforests. They are in danger if the forests are destroyed.

Sunniest place

The Sun shines the most in the Sahara Desert in North Africa.

Wettest place

It rains for 350 days every year on Mount Waialeale in the Hawaiian islands.

Coldest place

It is so cold at Vostok in Antarctica that your bare skin would freeze in seconds.

Driest place

Parts of the Atacama Desert in Chile have had no rain for over 400 years.

Glossary

canal
A waterway that is cut through land to join one place to another, so that goods can be carried between them by boat.
(pages 24, 25)

capital city
The most important city of a country. This is where the government of the country passes its laws.
(pages 13, 17, 22, 24, 26, 44, 45)

climate
The pattern of weather throughout the year in each part of the world, such as hot, sunny weather followed by cooler, rainy weather.
(pages 16, 31, 34, 36)

continent
One of seven large areas of land in the world: Africa, Antarctica, Asia, Australia, Europe, North America, and South America.
(pages 10, 11, 18, 38, 40)

crops
Plants that are grown by farmers to provide food for people. Crops are often sold to other countries. Each crop needs the right soil and climate to grow well.
(pages 16, 32, 34, 36)

earthquake
This is caused when large blocks of rock move beneath the surface of the earth. Cracks can open in the ground and buildings may collapse.
(page 22)

Equator
The imaginary line around the Earth, exactly halfway between the North and South Poles. Countries close to the

Equator are hot. Countries further away from the Equator are cooler.
(pages 10, 11, 12, 16)

farming
When people use land to grow crops or breed animals for food, or to produce materials such as wool, coffee, rubber, or tobacco.
(pages 17, 24, 25, 28, 29, 32, 34, 35, 36, 38)

fjord
A long, narrow bay or inlet in the rocky coast of Norway.
(page 27)

geyser
A water source, such as a spring, that shoots hot water high up into the air.
(pages 26, 41, 42)

hurricane
A violent storm with very strong winds that can cause a lot of damage to anything in its way.
(page 24)

industry
When goods are made or services are supplied. Different kinds of industry include factories, mines, and banks.
(pages 28, 29, 30)

island
A piece of land that is surrounded on all sides by water. Some islands are very small, such as Nauru; others are very large, such as Greenland.
(pages 18, 19, 22, 24, 30, 31, 37, 40, 41)

mine
A place where natural resources, such as coal, diamonds, or iron ore are dug from the ground.
(pages 28, 29, 38)

monsoon
A season of strong winds and heavy rain in countries around the northern part of the Indian Ocean.
(page 36)

plains
An area of flat, open land with only a few trees. Plains are often covered with grasslands.
(page 22)

port
A town or city on a sea coast with a harbour that is used to transport goods by sea.
(page 24)

prairie
A wide, treeless plain.
(page 20)

province
A particular area or division of a country or state.
(page 17, 21)

state
A large country can be split up into a number of states for administration purposes. For example, Nebraska and Iowa are two of the 50 states that make up the United States of America.
(pages 17, 22, 23)

terrain
An area of land, usually with a particular feature, such as mountains, plains, or rainforest.
(page 16)

territory
Land that belongs to a country or state.
(page 44)

volcano
A mountain or hill that is made up of ash and lava. Lava is hot, liquid rock from inside the Earth, which pours out from a crater when the volcano erupts.
(pages 22, 26, 37)

weather
Rain, wind, snow, fog, and sunshine are all different kinds of weather. Weather forecasts tell people how the weather is likely to change during the day.
(pages 16, 18, 30, 32, 41)

Country index

This index shows the pages on which you can find all the countries and their territories that are shown on the maps in this book. Each country is marked with its capital city.